ANDY THE LION AND FRIENDS

ISBN 979-8-89243-411-9 (paperback)
ISBN 979-8-89243-412-6 (digital)

Christian Faith Publishing
832 Park Avenue
Meadville, PA 16335
www.christianfaithpublishing.com

Printed in the United States of America

Andy the Lion and Friends

Showing the Love of God

ALISE MILES

Andy the Lion just woke up and started getting ready for the day. As he ate his breakfast, he read his verse of the day. It read:

A new command I give you: Love one another as I have loved you, so you must love one another. (John 13:34)

He finished his breakfast and walked out the door ready to do just that.

His first stop was at his best friend's, Alora Lamb's, house. She was outside in her garden. She loved to plant things and watch them grow. That was her favorite place to be. As he got closer, Andy noticed she was having some trouble and seemed to be upset.

"What's the matter, Miss Alora? Everything alright?" Andy asked.

"Oh, dear," said Alora. "No, it isn't. I have all these flowers to plant, and I just don't know how I'll get it done by myself."

"Don't worry, Alora. I'll help you," Andy said.

"Oh, thank you, Andy."

With Andy's help, they got it done very quickly. After he finished planting the last flower, he told Alora the Lamb farewell and walked to his next destination, which was Gideon Bear's house.

But as he went around the corner, Aubree Goat accidentally bumped into him. "Ooof!" Both fell on the sidewalk.

"Oh my!" yelled Skylar Donkey, "Are y'all okay?"

"*Yes, but watch where you're going!*" screamed Aubree.

Andy could see she was upset, and at first, he was too. But then he remembered his verse of the day to love one another. So he said, "Yes, I'm fine, and, Aubree, I'm sorry. It was an accident," and he helped her up.

Aubree started to smile and said, "I'm sorry I yelled. It wasn't your fault. Thank you for helping me up."

Andy said, "No worries, and you're welcome. Is there anything else I can help y'all with?"

Skylar Donkey said, "No, we are just on our way to the studio across the street to practice our dancing for our show."

"Oh, well have fun," replied Andy as he waved goodbye and continued on his way to Gideon Bear's house.

As he arrived at Gideon's house, he could hear music. At first, it was very catchy and had a good beat, but then you would hear a big screech that rang Andy's ears. He knocked on the door, but the music was so loud Gideon couldn't hear him, so he banged on the door louder. Finally, Gideon Bear opened the door.

"Oh, hello, Andy Lion. How's my friend doing today?"

"I'm doing very well, Gideon. I heard your music."

"Oh really?" replied Gideon. "How did it sound? Be honest."

Andy didn't want to lie to his friend but also didn't want to hurt his feelings. So he thought for a moment about his verse of the day and realized that telling the truth, but in a loving way, would be best.

"Well," Andy said, "it was good at the start, but then there was a screeching that hurt my ears at the end."

Gideon started to look a little disappointed. "Oh man, yeah, I can't seem to get that ending right," he said. "And I got to have it ready for Aubree and Skylar's dance show. What am I going to do?"

Andy thought for a moment, then had a wonderful idea. "Let's make up another ending. I'll help you, and I can play the drums."

"*That's a great idea, Andy!*" yelled Gideon.

They worked on the music for hours and finally came up with the perfect ending. After all that, Andy Lion was very tired and decided to go home. He brushed his teeth, got his PJs on, laid in bed, and said his prayer: "*Thank You, God, for giving me friends that I could love today.*"

The end.

ABOUT THE AUTHOR

I'm a Christian, a wife, and a mother of two small children. Like any parent, I want to make sure my kids have a strong foundation in Christ. That's why I wrote this book: to have God's word with examples of how to incorporate that into our children's lives.